Grammar, Punctuation and Spelling

PRACTICE QUESTIONS

Marie Lallaway

Acknowledgements

Rising Stars is grateful to the following schools who will be utilising Achieve to prepare their students for the National Tests: Chacewater Community Primary School, Cornwall; Coppice Primary School, Essex; Edgewood Primary School, Notts; Henwick Primary School, Eltham; Norwood Primary School, Southport; Sacred Heart Catholic Primary School, Manchester; Sunnyfields Primary School, Hendon; Tennyson Road Primary School, Luton.

ISBN: 978 1 78339 542 2

First published in 2015 by Rising Stars UK Ltd, part of Hodder Education, an Hachette UK Company
Reprinted 2016, 2017, 2018

Carmelite House

50 Victoria Embankment

London EC4Y 0DZ

www.risingstars-uk.com

Author: Marie Lallaway

Series Editor: Maddy Barnes

Accessibility Reviewer: Vivien Kilburn

Educational Adviser: Josh Lury

Publishers: Kate Jamieson and Gillian Lindsey

Project Manager: Estelle Lloyd

Editorial: Dodi Beardshaw, Rachel Evans, Amanda George, Fiona Leonard

Cover design: Burville-Riley Partnership

Text design and typeset by the Pen and Ink Book Company Ltd

Printed by Ashford Colour Press Ltd

A catalogue record for this title is available from the British Library.

Contents

Introduction 4

Grammar

Nouns 6
Adjectives 7
Adverbs 8
Modal verbs 9
Adverbials 10
Pronouns 11
Prepositions 12
Determiners 13
Conjunctions 14
Main clauses and subordinate clauses 15
Relative clauses 16
Noun phrases 17
Subject and object 18
Subject and verb agreement 19
Verbs in the progressive and perfect tenses 20
Passive and active voices 21
Subjunctive verb forms 22
Standard English and formality 23

Punctuation

Capital letters, full stops, exclamation marks and question marks 24
Commas 25
Inverted commas 26
Apostrophes 27
Parenthesis 28
Colons, semi-colons, single dashes, hyphens and bullet points 29

Spelling

Prefixes and suffixes 30
Prefixes 31
Suffixes: *-tion, -ssion, -cian* 32
Suffixes: *-ous, -tious, -cious* 33
Suffixes: *-able, -ably, -ible, -ibly* 34
Suffixes: *-ant, -ance, -ancy, -ent, -ence, -ency* 35
Words with *ie, ei, eigh, ey, ay* 36
Words with *ough* 37
Word endings: *al, el, il, le* 38
Silent letters 39
Homophones 40
Synonyms and antonyms 41
Word families 42

The answers can be found in a pull-out section in the middle of this book.

Welcome to Achieve Key Stage 2 GPS Practice Questions 100+

In this book you will find lots of practice and information to help you achieve 100+ in the Key Stage 2 English Grammar, Punctuation and Spelling (GPS) tests. You will look again at some of the same key knowledge that was in Achieve 100, but you will use it to tackle trickier questions and apply it in more complex ways.

About the Key Stage 2 Grammar, Punctuation and Spelling National Tests

The tests will take place in the summer term in Year 6. They will be done in your school and will be marked by examiners – not by your teacher.

The tests are divided into two papers:

Paper 1: questions – 45 minutes (50 marks)

- You will answer short questions about grammar, punctuation and language strategies.
- Some questions will ask you to tick a box, circle or underline. Other questions will ask you to add words to a sentence, or to rewrite it making a change. You may be asked to explain why a sentence is written in a particular way.
- The questions will include the language of grammar and punctuation.
- Most questions are worth 1 mark, but you should check to make sure before you answer each question in case you need to give more than one answer.

Paper 2: spelling – approximately 15 minutes (20 marks)

- Twenty questions will be read aloud to you, one at a time. You will be asked to spell a particular word in each sentence.
- The words may be taken from the word lists for Years 1–6.
- Each correct answer is worth 1 mark.

Test techniques

Before the tests

- Try to revise little and often, rather than in long sessions.
- Choose a time of day when you are not tired or hungry.
- Choose somewhere quiet so you can focus.
- Revise with a friend. You can encourage and learn from each other.
- Read the 'Top tips' throughout this book to remind you of important points in answering test questions.

During the tests

- READ THE QUESTION AND READ IT AGAIN.
- If you find a question difficult to answer, move on; you can always come back to it later.
- Always answer a multiple-choice question. If you really can't work out the answer, have a guess.
- Check to see how many marks a question is worth. Have you written enough to 'earn' those marks in your answer?
- Read the question again after you have answered it. Make sure you have given the correct number of answers within a question, e.g. 'Tick **two**'.
- If you have any time left at the end, go back to the questions you have missed. If you really do not know the answers, make guesses.

Where to get help:

- Pages 6–23 practise grammar.
- Pages 24–29 practise punctuation.
- Pages 30–42 practise spelling. (Note that in the test the words for you to spell will be read to you in a sentence. These pages cannot replicate that format, so instead they allow you to practise spelling lots of common words that might appear in the test.)
- The answers can be found in a pull-out section in the middle of this book.

Nouns

To achieve 100+ you need to know what nouns are and how to use them.

1 Write a sentence that uses the word <u>rush</u> as a **noun**. Remember to punctuate your answer correctly. 1 (1 mark)

It was in the morning. it was a rush

2 Tick two boxes to show which sentences below contain **nouns**. 2 (1 mark)

Tick **two**.

We have a strict bedtime routine. ☐
Can you give it to me later, please? ☐
She really likes you. ☐
Your rudeness is becoming a problem. ☐

3 Rewrite the sentence below, changing the **noun** for another that makes sense. Remember to punctuate your answer correctly. 3 (1 mark)

I understand your confusion.

____

4 Underline the **nouns** in the sentence below. 4 (1 mark)

The poem described a range of feelings such as love and hate.

5 Write the **nouns** that can be made from the verbs below. 5 (1 mark)

create ______________

intend ______________

pursue ______________

! Top tips

- Look out for adjectives that are similar to abstract nouns (e.g. *angry* and *anger*).
- Check if a word is an abstract noun by putting *the* in front of it (e.g. *the anger*, *the excitement*).

/5 Total for this page

Adjectives

To achieve 100+ you need to know what adjectives are and how to use them.

1 Circle all the **adjectives** in the sentence below.

The cheering crowds waved and smiled as the victorious team made a special procession through their home town.

1 (1 mark)

2 Tick one box in each row to show whether the underlined words are **adjectives** or **verbs**.

Sentence	Adjective	Verb
The <u>running</u> water overflowed the top of the bath.		
The dog <u>buried</u> a bone beneath the tree.		
You must <u>radio</u> for help as soon as you can.		
Never trust a <u>smiling</u> crocodile.		

2 (1 mark)

3 Underline **all** the **adjectives** in the passage below.

On our country walk, we spotted an unusually large bird. It sat upon a branch. When the bird stretched its wings, they were wider than my outstretched arms.

3 (1 mark)

4 Tick one box in each row to show whether the underlined words are **adjectives** or **adverbs**.

Sentence	Adjective	Adverb
Once we heard the new baby was born, we went <u>straight</u> to see her.		
This will be a great <u>advertising</u> opportunity for our product.		
In every competition someone has to come <u>first</u> and someone last.		

4 (1 mark)

! Top tip

- Decide what a word is doing in a sentence before deciding if it is an adjective.

/4 Total for this page

Adverbs

To achieve 100+ you need to know what adverbs are and how to use them.

1 Underline all the **adverbs** in this passage.

The curtains slowly opened and the stage was completely empty. The audience wondered what would happen next. Then, a small figure walked uncertainly to the centre of the stage.

☐ 1 *(1 mark)*

2 Tick three boxes to show which sentences contain **adverbs**.

Tick **three**.

The artist had carefully crafted a beautiful pot. ☐

We hope that you will have a safe journey. ☐

I hoped the phone would ring soon. ☐

How fast was the car travelling when it hit the tree? ☐

☐ 2 *(1 mark)*

3 Rewrite the sentence below, using a different **adverb**. Remember to punctuate your answer correctly.

You worked hard today.

____

☐ 3 *(1 mark)*

4 Tick one box in each row to show whether the underlined words are **adjectives** or **adverbs**.

Sentence	Adjective	Adverb
The tourist was <u>completely</u> confused by my directions.		
After a long list, the teacher finally gave the <u>last</u> instruction.		
Because he didn't listen to the directions, Sam took a <u>wrong</u> turn.		
You have done <u>well</u> to pass the test.		

☐ 4 *(1 mark)*

! Top tip

- **Watch out:** Don't miss common adverbs that refer to *when* something happens: *after, before, later, now, soon, yet*.

/4 *Total for this page*

Modal verbs

To achieve 100+ you need to know what modal verbs are and use them to show possibility.

1 Which of the events in the sentences below is **most** likely to happen?

Tick **one**.

The painter could fall from that ladder if he's not careful. ☐

I think Joe can score a goal in today's match. ☐

I will make you a lovely milkshake when we get home. ☐

We might have to cancel our walk if this rain persists. ☐

☐ 1 (1 mark)

2 Rewrite the sentence below, changing the **modal verb**. Remember to punctuate your answer correctly.

They will visit us tomorrow.

____

☐ 2 (1 mark)

3 Rewrite the sentence below, adding a **modal verb**. Remember to punctuate your answer correctly.

The ducks come if you throw them some bread.

____

____

☐ 3 (1 mark)

4 Underline the **modal verbs** in the sentence below.

We could go across the park to get to the station. It might not seem much of a shortcut, but we can run through the park, which is difficult to do on the pavement.

☐ 4 (1 mark)

/4 Total for this page

Adverbials

To achieve 100+ you need to identify and construct adverbials.

1 Circle the **adverbial phrase** in the sentence below.

If you wait, you'll see the bats that come out after dark.

(1 mark) 1

2 Add a suitable **adverbial** to complete the sentence below.

The museum opens a new exhibition ______________________.

(1 mark) 2

3 Rewrite the sentence below so that it has a fronted **adverbial**. Remember to use correct capital letters and punctuation.

Alice gritted her teeth and marched off with great determination.

____

(1 mark) 3

4 Explain the function of the underlined **adverbial** in the sentence below.

The weather had become worse <u>towards the end of the week</u>.

____

____

(1 mark) 4

5 Rewrite the sentence below, changing the position of the **adverbial**. Remember to punctuate your answer correctly.

Full of enthusiasm, the team ran out onto the pitch.

____

(1 mark) 5

! Top tip

- To help you find the adverbial, ask questions about the verb. *How? When? Where? Why?*

/5 *Total for this page*

Pronouns

To achieve 100+ you need to know what pronouns are and how to use them.

1 Tick one box in each row to show whether each sentence contains a **pronoun** or not.

Sentence	Pronoun	No pronoun
There are various theories about the extinction of dinosaurs.		
Spending too much time on a computer can give you a headache.		
Our boat leaves for France in two hours.		
They were able to take pictures of whales on their holiday.		

1 (1 mark)

2 Circle all the **pronouns** in the passage below.

Edward and Abigail were having a party. They had invited all of their friends. She wanted to play tennis but he would prefer party games.

2 (1 mark)

3 Tick one box to show the **pronouns** that complete the sentence below.

The musicians were tuning __________ instruments before __________ performance began so that __________ would be in tune.

our / a / us ☐ his / my / I ☐ your / their / it ☐ their / the / they ☐

3 (1 mark)

4 Explain why the underlined **pronoun** is used in the passage below.

Alexandra was ready for the match. <u>She</u> was looking forward to it.

____

4 (1 mark)

! Top tips

- **Watch out:** *It's* is a subject pronoun and a verb (e.g. *It's* (*It is*) *my birthday.*). *Its* is a possessive pronoun (e.g. *The car has lost its wheel.*).
- You can decide if a word is a pronoun by testing whether you can replace it with a noun.

/4 Total for this page

Prepositions

To achieve 100+ you need to know what prepositions are and be able to use them.

1 Circle **all** the **prepositions** in the sentence below.

Felix was sitting beside the teacher. He could see the park in the distance through the open window and imagined he was there, playing on the swings.

(1 mark) 1

2 Add a suitable **preposition** to the gaps in the passage below. Use each preposition only **once**.

The ducks are swimming ____________ the pond but the geese are feeding ____________ the trees, where people have dropped bread ____________ their sandwiches.

(1 mark) 2

3 Rewrite the sentence below, changing the **preposition**.

I put my book beneath my bed.

____

(1 mark) 3

4 Complete the sentence below, using *after* as a **preposition**.

I will finish my homework after ____________.

(1 mark) 4

5 Tick one box in each row to show whether the word <u>until</u> is used as a **preposition** or as a subordinating **conjunction**.

Sentence	**<u>until</u> used as a preposition**	**<u>until</u> used as a subordinating conjunction**
We can't leave for the airport <u>until</u> I find the passports.		
You can stay up <u>until</u> midnight on New Year's Eve.		
Sam is visiting his grandma <u>until</u> the weekend.		

(1 mark) 5

! Top tip

- **Watch out:** Some words can be used as both prepositions and conjunctions: *before, after, until.*

/5 Total for this page

Determiners

To achieve 100+ you need to know what determiners are and how to use them.

1 Add the correct **determiners** from the box to the passage below.

the	some	any

Alex wanted to make ______________ cakes but there weren't ______________ eggs in ______________ house.

1 (1 mark)

2 Underline **all** the **determiners** in the passage below.

These computer games are more fun than mine. I haven't bought any new ones lately so mine are old-fashioned.

2 (1 mark)

3 Tick two sentences that use <u>that</u> as a **determiner**.

Tick **two**.

You can't do <u>that</u>. ☐

Sam can carry <u>that</u> bag for you. ☐

<u>That</u> smoothie tastes delicious. ☐

The only bread <u>that</u> is left is mouldy. ☐

3 (1 mark)

4 Rewrite the sentence below, changing the **determiner**.
Remember to punctuate your answer correctly.

I really like these shoes.

____

4 (1 mark)

5 Circle all the **determiners** in the passage below.

The detectives couldn't find any evidence of a burglary so they returned to their police station.

5 (1 mark)

! Top tips

- **Watch out:** Some words can be pronouns and determiners. A determiner is used before a noun phrase; a pronoun is not (e.g. *please pass me that book* (determiner); *you can't do that* (pronoun)).
- Determiners that refer to quantity can be the hardest to spot.
- Always check through the use of all words that could be determiners.

/5

Total for this page

Conjunctions

To achieve 100+ you need to recognise and use the different conjunctions.

1 Tick one box in each row of the table to show whether the underlined words are **coordinating** or **subordinating conjunctions**.

1 (1 mark)

Sentence	Coordinating conjunction	Subordinating conjunction
The recent storms could have caused a lot of damage but we were very lucky.		
In Australia, visitors can trek up mountains or visit beautiful cities.		
At night, we can see lots of stars if the sky is clear.		
We can eat our sandwiches on the beach unless the tide is in.		

2 Underline all the **conjunctions** in the passage below.

2 (1 mark)

Insects can be fascinating when you study them. Because they are small, their beauty can be best appreciated under a microscope, or you could use a magnifying glass. However, some people are actually afraid of them.

3 Rewrite the sentence below, changing the **conjunction** for another that makes sense. Remember to punctuate your answer correctly.

3 (1 mark)

We can go swimming when you come to visit me.

4 Tick two boxes to show the sentences that are using the underlined words as **conjunctions**.

4 (1 mark)

Tick **two**.

The rain was heavy but we stayed dry. ☐

Don't open your presents until Christmas day. ☐

The musician left the stage after the applause finished. ☐

You should eat breakfast before school. ☐

/4 Total for this page

Main clauses and subordinate clauses

To achieve 100+ you need to recognise and use main and subordinate clauses.

1 Add the correct words to complete the **subordinate clauses** in the passage below.

if although which

The museum has a variety of exciting exhibitions __________ the most popular is the Roman village __________ is located on the ground floor. School groups are invited to dress up in Roman clothing __________ the pupils would like to do so.

1 (1 mark)

2 Underline the **subordinate clause** in the sentence below.

I become nervous whenever I have to speak to the whole class.

2 (1 mark)

3 Tick one box in each row to show whether the underlined clause is a **main clause** or a **subordinate clause**.

Sentence	Main clause	Subordinate clause
The summer weather is usually warm although sometimes we get rain.		
If you scatter breadcrumbs on the grass, the ducks will come out of the pond.		
We won't need to bring wellies unless it rains.		
Picking up litter is a school rule.		

3 (1 mark)

4 Rewrite the sentence below to place the **subordinate clause** first. Remember to punctuate your answer correctly.

I will help you if you will let me.

____

4 (1 mark)

! Top tips

- Do the clauses make a complete sentence on their own? If so, they are main clauses. If not, they are subordinate clauses.
- A subordinate clause begins with a subordinating conjunction such as *while, if, when, because.*

/4

Total for this page

Relative clauses

To achieve 100+ you need to recognise and use relative clauses.

1 Which of these sentences contain a **relative clause**? 1 (1 mark)

Tick **two**.

- While the class watched, the scientist conducted an experiment. ☐
- The telephone rang just as we were about to leave the house. ☐
- The acrobat who is wearing the red shirt is the best. ☐
- The house in which my grandad lives is over 300 years old. ☐

2 Add the correct **relative pronouns** to the passage below. 2 (1 mark)

who that when

The photograph __________ is hanging in the school hall reminds us of the day __________ the Queen came to visit. All the visitors __________ walk past it comment on it.

3 Tick one box in each row of the table to show whether the word <u>that</u> is used to introduce a **relative clause** or as a **determiner**. 3 (1 mark)

Sentence	**<u>that</u> used to introduce a relative clause**	**<u>that</u> used as a determiner**
The judge preferred <u>that</u> picture to this one.		
Games of chess <u>that</u> last for hours are hard work.		
I would like to watch <u>that</u> film at the weekend.		
The door <u>that</u> leads to the fire escape should never be locked.		

! Top tip

- *That* is not always a relative pronoun. It can be a determiner (see page 13), (e.g. I like *that* picture). To check whether it begins a relative clause, check if it is followed by a verb (e.g. I like the picture *that is hanging in the hall*).

/3 Total for this page

Noun phrases

To achieve 100+ you need to recognise and use noun phrases.

1 Underline all the words that make the **noun phrase** in the sentence below. 1 (1 mark)

The sprinting cheetah was travelling incredibly fast.

2 Circle all the **noun phrases** in the sentence below. 2 (1 mark)

While a crescent moon hung in the sky, wolves' cries echoed through the forest.

3 Expand the underlined **noun phrase** in the sentence below. Write the new phrase on the line below. 3 (1 mark)

<u>The waves</u> crashed onto the beach during the storm.

____

4 Rewrite the sentence below, adding to the **noun phrase**. Remember to punctuate your answer correctly. 4 (1 mark)

I saw some butterflies yesterday.

____

5 Which of the sentences below contain **noun phrases**? 5 (1 mark)

Tick **two**.

Large dogs are not allowed in the playground. ☐

Please give it to me. ☐

Finlay took his brother's new computer game. ☐

You are taller and stronger than me. ☐

/5 Total for this page

Subject and object

To achieve 100+ you need to identify the subject and object of sentences.

1 Write **S** (**subject**) and **O** (**object**) in the boxes below the sentence below.

1 (1 mark)

Josh was making faces at the monkeys in the zoo, but they did not copy him.

2 Rewrite the sentence below, changing the **object**. Remember to punctuate your answer correctly.

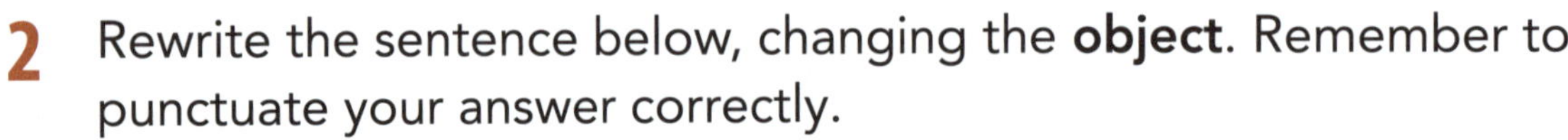

2 (1 mark)

The rabbits escaped from the hutch.

____

3 Circle all the **subjects** in the passage below.

3 (1 mark)

While he was waiting for his mum, Oscar listened to the radio in the car. Alysha, his favourite singer, was talking to the presenter about her music.

4 Underline the **object** in the sentence below.

4 (1 mark)

Sheena had been hit by a stray football in the playground.

5 Tick one box in each row to show whether Kazim is a **subject** or an **object** in the sentences below.

5 (1 mark)

Sentence	Subject	Object
I can't see Kazim anywhere.		
If Kazim studies hard, he'll pass the test.		
We'll collect Kazim on our way to school.		
Kazim was being pushed along by the crowd.		

/5

Total for this page

Subject and verb agreement

To achieve 100+ you need to make the subject and verb of a sentence agree.

1 Tick the sentences that are correct.

Spring flowers are beginning to bloom in the garden. ☐

At the opening ceremony, each team of competitors marches past the judges. ☐

Members of the local council is coming to visit our school next week. ☐

Children should enter through the doors near the playground. ☐

1 ☐ (1 mark)

2 Circle the correct words to complete the sentences below.

Although a bunch of flowers make / makes a lovely 'thank you' gift for a teacher, some people prefer / prefers a box of chocolates. However, my teacher like / likes a drawing or a poem to remind her of us.

2 ☐ (1 mark)

3 Write is or are in the gaps in the sentences below to make the **subject** and **verb** agree.

A swarm of wasps ______________ gathering in the roof of our house.

The government ______________ led by the Prime Minister.

A school of dolphins ______________ swimming near our boat.

Police officers ______________ trained to deal with difficult situations.

3 ☐ (1 mark)

- Focus on the first part of the noun phrase, e.g. *herd* of goats, *collections* of pictures, to know whether to use a plural or singular verb form.

/3 Total for this page

Verbs in the progressive and perfect tenses

To achieve 100+ you need to recognise the present and past progressive tenses and the present and past perfect tenses and be able to construct these verb forms.

1 Fill in the gaps in the sentence below, using the **past progressive** form of the verbs in the boxes.

to work

While I was working hard on my homework, my sister

to relax

was ~~relaxed~~ relaxing on the sofa watching television.

(1 mark) 1

2 Fill in the gaps in the sentence below, using the **present perfect** form of the verbs in the boxes.

to learn

Leo learnt his lines for the school play and his dad

to help

helped him to make his costume.

(1 mark) 2

3 In the sentence below, Ella laid the table before she changed for her party. Complete the sentence with the correct verb form.

to lay

After Ella had laid the table, she changed for her party.

(1 mark) 3

4 Tick the boxes that show the sentences that contain verbs in the **progressive forms**.

My headache is hurting a lot this afternoon. ☑

I always have a shower before I go to bed. ☐

The seals were waiting for the keepers to feed them. ☑

All of the children ran out to play in the snow. ☐

(1 mark) 4

3 /4

Total for this page

Passive and active voices

To achieve 100+ you need to recognise the active and passive voices.

1 Tick one box in each row of the table to show whether each sentence is in the **active** or the **passive** voice.

Sentence	Active	Passive
The police were quickly called to the accident on the motorway.		
Planes were flying low and doing stunts at the air show.		
A new treatment for flu has been discovered by international scientists.		
The vets at the surgery are busy helping to deliver a litter of kittens.		

1 (1 mark)

2 Which option completes the sentence below in the **passive** voice?

Despite his best efforts, Tristan

Tick **one**.

lost the match. ☐

was beaten. ☐

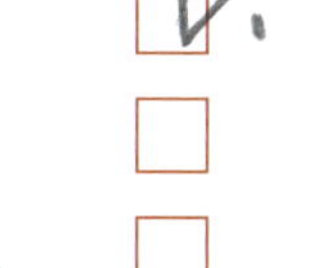

could not win the match. ☐

would have to play another match. ☐

2 (1 mark)

3 Rewrite the sentence below in the **passive** voice. Remember to punctuate your answer correctly.

A gust of wind blew shut the window.

3 (1 mark)

4 Rewrite the sentence below in the **active** voice. Remember to punctuate your answer correctly.

The remains of the cake were eaten by the dog.

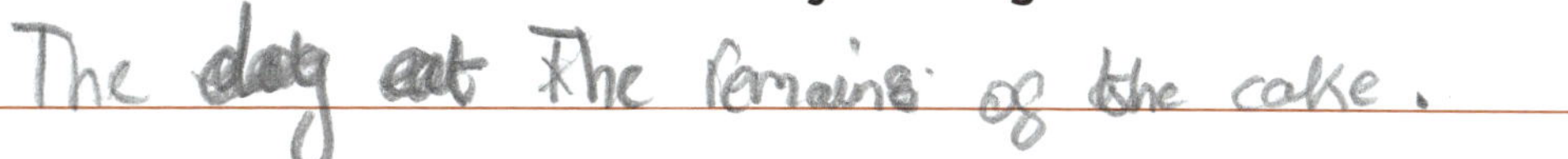

4 (1 mark)

3 /4

Total for this page

Subjunctive verb forms

To achieve 100+ you need to recognise verbs in the subjunctive form.

1 Which option completes the sentence below so that it uses the **subjunctive** mood?

Billy wished he _______________ able to run as fast as his sister.

Tick **one**.

were ☐ was ☐ could be ☐ may be ☐

1 (1 mark)

2 Write the correct form of the verb in the gap below so that it uses the **subjunctive** mood.

to clean

The dentist recommended that Elisha _______________ her teeth more thoroughly to avoid a filling.

2 (1 mark)

3 Which of the sentences below is written in the **subjunctive** mood?

The astronomer had been able to see a shooting star as the night was so clear. ☐

If you are here on time, you will be able to watch the start of the film. ☐

Jessica's grandad suggested that she save a little money each week for her holiday. ☐

While Joe was clearing up, his brother just played on the computer. ☐

3 (1 mark)

4 Rewrite the verb underlined in the sentence below so that it uses the **subjunctive** mood.

Eddie's teacher insisted that he <u>wears</u> school uniform the same as anyone else. _______________

4 (1 mark)

5 Rewrite the sentence below so that it uses the **subjunctive** mood. Remember to punctuate your answer correctly.

I would get that cut looked at by a doctor if I was you.

____

5 (1 mark)

/5 Total for this page

Answers

All answers are worth 1 mark, unless otherwise indicated.

Nouns (page 6)

1 Accept a sentence that makes sense, using 'rush' as a noun, e.g. I was in a great rush. The sentence must be correctly punctuated.

2 tick: We have a strict bedtime routine.
Your rudeness is becoming a problem.

3 Accept answers that change the noun 'confusion' for another that makes sense, e.g. problem; idea; question. The sentence must be correctly punctuated.

4 underline: poem; range; feelings; love; hate

5 creation; intention; pursuit

Adjectives (page 7)

1 circle: cheering; victorious; special; home

2 The running water overflowed the top of the bath. adjective
The dog buried a bone beneath the tree. verb
You must radio for help as soon as you can. verb
Never trust a smiling crocodile. adjective

3 underline: country; large; wider; outstretched

4 Once we heard the new baby was born, we went straight to see her. adverb
This will be a great advertising opportunity for our product. adjective
In every competition someone has to come first and someone last. adverb

Adverbs (page 8)

1 underline: slowly; completely; next; Then; uncertainly

2 tick: The artist had carefully crafted a beautiful pot.
I hoped the phone would ring soon.
How fast was the car travelling when it hit the tree?

3 Accept answers that change 'hard' for another adverb, e.g. well; quickly; poorly. The sentence must be correctly punctuated.

4 The tourist was completely confused by my directions. adverb
After a long list, the teacher finally gave the last instruction. adjective
Because he didn't listen to the directions, Sam took a wrong turn. adjective
You have done well to pass the test. adverb

Modal verbs (page 9)

1 tick: I will make you a lovely milkshake when we get home.

2 Accept answers that change the verb 'will' for another modal, e.g. must; should; could; may; might. The sentence must be correctly punctuated.

3 Accept answers that add a modal verb before 'come', e.g. may, could, might, will. The sentence must be correctly punctuated.

4 underline: could; might; can

Adverbials (page 10)

1 circle: after dark

2 Accept answers that give an adverbial and make sense, e.g. at the end of the month; in the top gallery.

3 With great determination, Alice gritted her teeth and marched off. The sentence must be correctly punctuated.

4 Accept answers that refer to the adverbial giving information about time, e.g. it tells you when it happens.

5 The team ran out onto the pitch, full of enthusiasm./The team, full of enthusiasm, ran out onto the pitch. The sentence must be correctly punctuated.

Pronouns (page 11)

1 There are various theories about the extinction of dinosaurs. no pronoun
Spending too much time on a computer can give you a headache. pronoun
Our boat leaves for France in two hours. no pronoun
They were able to take pictures of whales on their holiday. pronoun

2 circle: They; their; She; he

3 tick: their; the; they

4 Accept answers that explain that the pronoun avoids repetition of the name.

Prepositions (page 12)

1 circle: beside; in; through; on

2 Accept suitable answers, e.g. in the pond; beside/beneath/between the trees; from their sandwiches.

3 Accept suitable answers that make sense, e.g. on; below; beside.

4 Accept answers that follow 'after' with a noun or noun phrase, e.g. lunch; the programme. Do not accept answers that contain a verb, e.g. after I eat my supper.

5 We can't leave for the airport until I find the passports. subordinating conjunction
You can stay up until midnight on New Year's Eve. preposition
Sam is visiting his grandma until the weekend. preposition

Determiners (page 13)

1 some; any; the

2 underline: These; any

3 tick: Sam can carry that bag for you.
That smoothie tastes delicious.

4 I really like those/the/any shoes. The sentence must be correctly punctuated.

5 circle: The; any; a

Conjunctions (page 14)

1 The recent storms could have caused a lot of damage but we were very lucky. coordinating conjunction
In Australia, visitors can trek up mountains or visit beautiful cities. coordinating conjunction
At night, we can see lots of stars if the sky is clear. subordinating conjunction
We can eat our sandwiches on the beach unless the tide is in. subordinating conjunction

2 underline: when; Because; or

3 Accept answers that change the conjunction and make sense, e.g. if; as soon as; whenever. The sentence must be correctly punctuated.

4 tick: The musician left the stage after the applause finished.
The rain was heavy but we stayed dry.

Main clauses and subordinate clauses (page 15)

1 although; which; if
2 underline: whenever I have to speak to the whole class
3 The summer weather is usually warm although sometimes we get rain. main clause
If you scatter breadcrumbs on the grass, the ducks will come out of the pond. subordinate clause
We won't need to bring wellies unless it rains. subordinate clause
Picking up litter is a school rule. main clause
4 If you will let me, I will help you. The sentence must be correctly punctuated.

Relative clauses (page 16)

1 tick: The acrobat who is wearing the red shirt is the best.
The house in which my grandad lives is over 300 years old.
2 that; when; who
3 The judge preferred that picture to this one. determiner
Games of chess that last for hours are hard work. relative clause
I would like to watch that film at the weekend. determiner
The door that leads to the fire escape should never be locked. relative clause

Noun phrases (page 17)

1 underline: The sprinting cheetah
2 circle: a crescent moon; in the sky; wolves' cries; through the forest
3 Accept answers that expand 'the waves', e.g. The violent/enormous waves…
4 Accept answers that expand 'butterflies' and make sense, e.g. I saw some beautiful/large/unusual butterflies yesterday. The sentence must be correctly punctuated.
5 tick: Large dogs are not allowed in the playground.
Finlay took his brother's new computer game.

Subject and object (page 18)

1 Josh: subject; monkeys: object; they: subject; him: object
2 Accept suitable answers that change 'hutch' for another object, e.g. The rabbits escaped from the fox/cage/terrible storm.
The sentence must be correctly punctuated.
3 circle: he; Oscar; Alysha
4 underline: a stray football
5 I can't see Kazim anywhere. object
If Kazim studies hard, he'll pass the test. subject
We'll collect Kazim on our way to school. object
Kazim was being pushed along by the crowd. object

Subject and verb agreement (page 19)

1 tick: Spring flowers are beginning to bloom in the garden.
At the opening ceremony, each team of competitors marches past the judges.
Children should enter through the doors near the playground.
2 circle: makes; prefer; likes
3 is; is; is; are

Verbs in the progressive and perfect tenses (page 20)

1 was working; was relaxing
2 has learned; has helped
3 had laid/had lain
4 tick: My headache is hurting a lot this afternoon.
The seals were waiting for the keepers to feed them.

Passive and active voices (page 21)

1 The police were quickly called to the accident on the motorway. passive
Planes were flying low and doing stunts at the air show. active
A new treatment for flu has been discovered by international scientists. passive
The vets at the surgery are busy helping to deliver a litter of kittens. active
2 tick: was beaten.
3 The window was/has been blown shut by a gust of wind. The sentence must be correctly punctuated.
4 The dog ate/has eaten the remains of the cake. The sentence must be correctly punctuated.

Subjunctive verb forms (page 22)

1 tick: were
2 clean
3 tick: Jessica's grandad suggested that she save a little money each week for her holiday.
4 wear
5 I would get that cut looked at by a doctor if I were you. The sentence must be correctly punctuated.

Standard English and formality (page 23)

1 circle: that; did
2 I have fewer sweets than you. The sentence must be correctly punctuated.
3 circle: confirm
4 Accept an answer that recognises an increase in formality, e.g. The second one is more formal./The first one is informal and the second is formal.
5 I haven't/have not got anything for you./I have nothing for you. The sentence must be correctly punctuated.

Capital letters, full stops, exclamation marks and question marks (page 24)

1 tick: In the autumn, Heath School will teach Chinese and art.
2 circle: kim; precious pets; april; norris street
3 Christmas: because it is the name of a festival. Scotland: because it is the name of a place/country.
4 Accept answers that refer to the exclamation mark conveying surprise or enthusiasm. Do not accept answers that refer to loudness.

Commas (page 25)

1 tick: to mark a clause
2 Alfie uses a powerful telescope to see the night sky, the moon and the stars. Whenever the night is clear, he looks at the stars.
3 Now that I've heard the explanation I understand, Lucy.
4 Packing the shopping carefully, placing items, such as the eggs, on the top, the twins were showing how sensible they could be.
5 Accept answers that show understanding that the comma affects whether Mark is being spoken about, or spoken to directly.

Inverted commas (page 26)

1 tick: "Could dragons once have walked the earth, like dinosaurs?" wondered Angel.
Angel wondered, "Could dragons once have walked the earth, like dinosaurs?"

2 "Don't forget to fill up with fuel before your journey," reminded Mum.
The sentence must be correctly punctuated.

3 tick: "Hurry up," called Elizabeth, "or we will be late."
Peter asked if the game had already started.

4 "The burglar has not managed to steal anything, despite the broken window," said the police officer.
The police officer said, "The burglar has not managed to steal anything, despite the broken window."
The sentence must be correctly punctuated.

Apostrophes (page 27)

1 He couldn't climb the wall. missing letter
That is the dog's bowl. possession
Let's go to your house. missing letter
It's my turn. missing letter

2 circle: Ive; childrens; wont

3 Today's sunshine isn't expected at this time of year but it's very welcome.
The sentence must be correctly punctuated.

4 wouldn't: apostrophe used for contraction/to replace a missing letter.
John's: apostrophe used to show possession/belonging to someone.

Parenthesis (page 28)

1 tick: James, despite being the chattiest boy in the class, still managed to complete his work on time.

2 When we go on safari, I hope to see some big animals – maybe an elephant, rhino or hippo – and take photos.

3 Before we leave on holiday, my dad goes through his checklist (passport, tickets, toothbrush) as he starts the car.

4 tick: Clowns are popular with some people, but – perhaps surprisingly – others find them rather scary.
Please buy your tickets (available from May 20th) from the booking office or online.

5 Accept answers that show that parenthesis is used to add extra information about 'the family', e.g. it tells who is in the family.

Colons, semi-colons, single dashes, hyphens and bullet points (page 29)

1 tick: Daniel went to the doctor's with a dreadful cough; he was given medicine to take daily.

2 At the weekend, we went to the beach and looked for interesting stones beneath the cliffs – it was a lovely day.

3 Accept answers that use bullet points with consistent punctuation, e.g. with no punctuation on each line, or with commas/semi-colons on each and a full stop on the last.
To make your cake, you will need these ingredients:
- eggs
- sugar
- butter
- flour

4 For her birthday, we bought my grandma her favourite flowers: daffodils, tulips and roses.

Prefixes and suffixes (page 30)

1 anti

2 joyfulness; direction, directness; builder, building

3 dis

4 autograph; subaqua; aquamarine

5 Accept any word ending in *-ness*, e.g. plainness; sadness.

Prefixes (page 31)

1 Accept sentences that use these words appropriately: disappointment; disarm; disconnect; discourage; dishonourable.
The sentences must be correctly punctuated.

2 a) disclose; b) discontented; c) detained; d) destruction; e) desolate

3 a) inexcusable
b) impertinent
c) irreverent
d) imperfect
e) illegal
f) illogical
g) impossible
h) indirect

Suffixes: *-tion, -ssion, -cian* (page 32)

1 Ends in d, de or se:

apprehend	apprehension
persuade	persuasion
ascend	ascension
decide	decision
extend	extension
confuse	confusion

Ends in c or cs:

politic	politician
electric	electrician

Ends in ss or mit:

permit	permission
express	expression
possess	possession

Ends in another way:

divert	diversion
exhibit	exhibition
inject	injection

2 a) repetition; b) adaptation; c) expulsion; d) evolution

Suffixes: *-ous, -tious, -cious* (page 33)

1

boisterous	lively
callous	hard-hearted
carnivorous	meat-eating
conscious	awake
cautious	careful
momentous	important
courteous	well-mannered

2 Accept sentences that use these words appropriately: infectious; religious; notorious; outrageous. The sentences must be correctly punctuated.

3 furious; various; glorious; studious; injurious

Suffixes: *-able, -ably, -ible, -ibly* (page 34)

1 a) plausible; b) unreachable; c) unintelligible; d) edible; e) irreversible

2 unnoticeable; probably; unbelievable; flexible

3 classifiable; identifiable; reliable; enviable; glorifiable; pitiable.
Accept sentences that use these words appropriately.

Suffixes: *-ant, -ance, -ancy, -ent, -ence, -ency* (page 35)

1 preference — choice
advance — go forwards
magnificent — wonderful
conference — meeting
existence — life
incompetence — failure

2 absent; diligently; performance; audience; interference; persistently

3 circle: transparent; acquaintance; resistance; perseverance; vigilant; insignificant

Words with *ie, ei, eigh, ey, ay* (page 36)

1 a) achievement; b) convenient; c) courier; d) niece; e) fiercely

2 *ei* words:
ceiling
protein
counterfeit
deceitful
Einstein
foreigner
height
heiress
ie words:
alien
hygienic
relieve
field

3 a) heiress; b) counterfeit; c) Einstein; d) hygienic; e) foreigner

Words with *ough* (page 37)

1 a) enough; b) boughs; c) hiccoughs; d) wrought; e) afterthought; f) drought

2 roughness/est/en; thoroughness; toughness/est/en; thoughtlessness

3 brougham — a type of horse-drawn carriage
thoroughfare — a roadway
doughty — hardy, brave
furlough — a period of leave for a soldier
slough off — get rid of
thoroughbred — a type of racehorse

Word endings: *al, el, il, le* (page 38)

1 anvil — a blacksmith's tool
uncivil — impolite
abnormal — unusual
cardinal — a high-status job in the church
admiral — an officer in the navy
satchel — a type of bag

2 fossil; aerial; applicable; coastal; presidential; professional; icicle; sentimental; carousel; mythical; barrel; terrible; parallel; archaeological; squirrel

3 audible; criminal; peril; carousel

Silent letters (page 39)

1 a) handkerchief; b) scene; c) scissors; d) hymn; e) crumb; f) fascinate; g) campaign; h) solemn; i) guilt

2 a) whistle; b) guess; c) gnome; d) tomb; e) crescent; f) design; g) sandwich; h) listen; i) knowledge; j) rogue

3 Accept sentences that make sense. The sentences must be correctly punctuated.

Homophones (page 40)

1 a) board; b) desert; c) accept; d) queue; e) stationary

2 loan — lone
maid — made
bawled — bald/balled
bear — bare
alter — altar
seam — seem
sighed — side
sole — soul

3 a) maize; b) mist; c) seize; d) sort; e) shake

Synonyms and antonyms (page 41)

1 tick: agree

2 wandering — direct
aggressive — pacifying
achieve — abandon
durable — weak

3 tick: confirm

4 tick: old-fashioned

5 comply — agree
coerce — persuade
corrupt — destroy
collate — organise

Word families (page 42)

1 tick: correspondent; correspondence

2 deliver

3 improved/improvement/improvable

4 tick: hide

5 Accept an answer that uses 'curve' as a noun and makes sense, e.g. I drew a curve on my diagram. The sentence must be correctly punctuated.

6 Accept an answer that uses 'curve' as a verb and makes sense, e.g. The road curved around the hillside. The sentence must be correctly punctuated.

Standard English and formality

To achieve 100+ you need to know how to identify and use Standard English, and to identify differences between informal and formal language.

1 Circle one word in each underlined pair to complete the sentences using **Standard English**.

I would like the cake <u>that / what</u> is in the window.

We all <u>did / done</u> our work in extra quick time.

1 (1 mark)

2 Rewrite the sentence below using **Standard English**. Remember to punctuate your answer correctly.

I have less sweets than you.

2 (1 mark)

3 Circle the word to complete the sentence using the most **formal** language.

The office will telephone you to <u>give / confirm</u> the time of your appointment.

3 (1 mark)

4 Explain the effect of changing the words underlined in the sentences below.

Archie gave a speech to express his <u>thanks</u> for the prize.

Archie gave a speech to express his <u>gratitude</u> for the prize.

4 (1 mark)

5 Rewrite the sentence below using **Standard English**. Remember to punctuate your answer correctly.

I ain't got nothing for you.

5 (1 mark)

/5

Total for this page

Capital letters, full stops, exclamation marks and question marks

To achieve 100+ you need to use capital letters, full stops, exclamation marks and question marks in the right places in sentences.

1 Which sentence uses **capital letters** correctly?

Tick **one**.

In the Autumn, Heath School will teach Chinese and art. ☐

In the Autumn, Heath school will teach Chinese and art. ☐

In the Autumn, Heath School will teach Chinese and Art. ☐

In the autumn, Heath School will teach Chinese and art. ☐

1 *(1 mark)*

2 Circle the words that should have **capital letters** in the passage below.

Our cousin, kim, is opening a new business called precious pets. It will open at the end of spring, in april, in a shop on norris street.

2 *(1 mark)*

3 Explain why the words underlined should have a **capital letter**.

At <u>Christmas</u> we will be going to visit our cousins in <u>Scotland</u>.

Christmas ______________________________

Scotland ______________________________

3 *(1 mark)*

4 Explain how the use of the **exclamation mark** changes the effect of the sentence below.

You have passed your driving test – how clever.

You have passed your driving test – how clever!

____

4 *(1 mark)*

! Top tip

- Remember that all parts of proper nouns need capital letters (e.g. *Sally Smith, United Kingdom, Rising Stars Publications*).

/4 *Total for this page*

Commas

To achieve 100+ you need to use commas to mark clauses or phrases, to separate items in a list and to clarify meanings.

1 Tick one box to show why **commas** have been used in the sentence below.

Unless the fire engine arrives soon, the flames will destroy the shed.

Tick **one**.

to introduce a piece of speech ☐

to mark a clause ☐

to separate items in a list ☐

to separate two sentences ☐

1 (1 mark)

2 Add **commas** to the passage below.

Alfie uses a telescope to see the night sky the moon and the stars. Whenever the night is clear he looks at the stars.

2 (1 mark)

3 Insert a **comma** to demonstrate that the speaker is talking directly to Lucy.

Now that I've heard the explanation I understand Lucy.

3 (1 mark)

4 Insert **commas** in the sentence below.

Packing the shopping carefully placing items such as the eggs on the top the twins were showing how sensible they could be.

4 (1 mark)

5 Explain how a **comma** changes the meaning of the sentence below.

Will you help, Mark?
Will you help Mark?

____

____

5 (1 mark)

! Top tips

- Remember to use two commas to mark an embedded clause or phrase (e.g. *Oscar, my favourite cat, often sits on my shoulder.*).
- Look out for adverbial phrases and clauses that require a comma (e.g. *Suddenly, I saw it. Next, it saw me.*).

/5 Total for this page

Inverted commas

To achieve 100+ you need to use inverted commas to show direct speech.

1 Which of the sentences below are correctly punctuated? Tick **two**.

"Could dragons once have walked the earth, like dinosaurs?" wondered Angel. ☐

Angel wondered, "Could dragons once have walked the earth, like dinosaurs"? ☐

"Could dragons once have walked the earth, like dinosaurs," wondered Angel? ☐

Angel wondered, "Could dragons once have walked the earth, like dinosaurs?" ☐

1 *(1 mark)*

2 Rewrite the sentence below, using correct punctuation for **direct speech**.

Don't forget to fill up with fuel before your journey reminded Mum

____

2 *(1 mark)*

3 Which of the sentences below are correctly punctuated?

"Hurry up," called Elizabeth, "or we will be late." ☐

Zach wanted to know "when he was supposed to begin the game?" ☐

Peter asked if the game had already started. ☐

"If you continue to blow up that balloon" warned Ali, "it will burst." ☐

3 *(1 mark)*

4 Rewrite the sentence below, putting the police officer's words into **direct speech**. Remember to punctuate your answer correctly.

The police officer said that the burglar had not managed to steal anything despite the broken window.

____

____

4 *(1 mark)*

! Top tip

- If you place the commas first, it is easier to make sure they are correctly inside or outside the speech marks.

/4

Total for this page

Apostrophes

To achieve 100+ you need to use apostrophes correctly.

1 Tick one box in each row to show how the **apostrophe** has been used in the sentence. 1 (1 mark)

Sentence	To replace a missing letter	To show possession
He couldn't climb the wall.		
That is the dog's bowl.		
Let's go to your house.		
It's my turn.		

2 Circle the words in the sentence below that should be written with **apostrophes**. 2 (1 mark)

Ive left the childrens coats behind so they wont be able to go outside.

3 Rewrite the sentence below, correctly using **apostrophes**. 3 (1 mark)

Todays sunshine isnt expected at this time of year but its very welcome.

____

____

4 Explain why **apostrophes** are used in the sentence below. 4 (1 mark)

I wouldn't believe everything that John's brother says.

wouldn't ______________________________

John's ______________________________

! Top tips

- Beware of words that join together or change when the apostrophe is added (e.g. *could not* = *couldn't*; *will not* = *won't*).
- **Watch out:** *Its* and *it's* are often confused. *It's* is *it is* shortened. *Its* is used for possession. There is no apostrophe in *its*, for possession.
- **Watch out:** Apostrophes of possession can be tricky with plurals (e.g. *Foxes' tails are bushy* but *The fox's tail was injured.*).

/4 Total for this page

Parenthesis

To achieve 100+ you need to recognise the correct use of a parenthesis.

1 Which of these sentences uses **commas** correctly? Tick **one**.

James despite being the chattiest boy, in the class, still managed to complete his work on time. ☐

James despite being the chattiest boy in the class, still managed to complete his work, on time. ☐

James, despite being the chattiest boy in the class, still managed to complete his work on time. ☐

James, despite being the chattiest boy in the class still managed to complete his work, on time. ☐

1 (1 mark)

2 Rewrite the sentence below, correctly adding two **dashes**.

When we go on safari, I hope to see some big animals maybe an elephant, rhino or hippo and take photos.

____

____

2 (1 mark)

3 Add **brackets** to the sentence below.

Before we leave on holiday, my dad goes through his checklist passport, tickets, toothbrush as he starts the car.

3 (1 mark)

4 Which sentences are correctly punctuated? Tick **two**.

The tight-rope walker, wobbled wildly, on the wire. ☐

Clowns are popular with some people, but – perhaps surprisingly – others find them rather scary. ☐

Please buy your tickets (available from May 20th) from the booking office or online. ☐

The gymnasts tumbled around the circus ring (to the delight) of the audience. ☐

4 (1 mark)

5 Explain why **parenthesis** has been used in the sentence below.

Many members of the family (grandparents, cousins, aunts and uncles) are coming to the party.

____

5 (1 mark)

/5

Total for this page

Colons, semi-colons, single dashes, hyphens and bullet points

To achieve 100+ you need to recognise and use these punctuation marks correctly.

1 Tick one box to show the sentence that is correctly punctuated.

Tick **one**.

Daniel went to the doctor's; with a dreadful cough. He was given medicine to take daily. ☐

Daniel went to the doctor's with a dreadful cough; he was given medicine to take daily. ☐

Daniel; went to the doctor's with a dreadful cough. He was given medicine to take daily. ☐

Daniel went to the doctor's with a dreadful cough, He was given medicine to take; daily. ☐

1 (1 mark)

2 Add a **single dash** to the sentence below.

At the weekend, we went to the beach and looked for interesting stones beneath the cliffs it was a lovely day.

2 (1 mark)

3 **To make a cake, Benny needs four ingredients: eggs, sugar, butter and flour.**

Finish the recipe below, writing the ingredients as a list with **bullet points**.

To make your cake, you will need these ingredients:

____

____

____

____

3 (1 mark)

4 Rewrite the information below, correctly using a **colon**.

For her birthday, we bought my grandma her favourite flowers (daffodils, tulips and roses).

____

____

4 (1 mark)

/4 Total for this page

Prefixes and suffixes

To achieve 100+ you need to add prefixes and suffixes to words.

1 Which **prefix** can be added to both of the words below? 1 (1 mark)

______septic

______social

Prefix: ______________

2 Add **suffixes** to make these words into nouns. 2 (1 mark)

joyful______________

direct______________

build______________

3 Which **prefix** can be added to both of the words below? 3 (1 mark)

charge

qualify

Prefix: ______________

4 Add a **prefix** from the box to each of the words below to make a new word. 4 (1 mark)

Use each prefix only once.

aqua	**sub**	**auto**

______graph

______aqua

______marine

5 Write a word that has the same **suffix** as the word below. 5 (1 mark)

forgiveness

____

/5 *Total for this page*

Prefixes

To achieve 100+ you need to correctly spell words with prefixes.

1 Add the dis **prefix** to these words to make new words. Write a sentence for each one. Remember to punctuate your answers correctly.

appointment ______________________

arm ______________________

connect ______________________

courage ______________________

honourable ______________________

1 (1 mark)

2 Circle the correct spelling in each sentence.

a) You must **disclose / desclose** any information you have about the crime.

b) Alfie has always been a **discontented / descontented** child.

c) The robber has been **ditained / detained** by the police.

d) The earthquake caused much **destruction / distruction**.

e) After the fire, the landscape lay **desolate / disolate** and bare.

2 (1 mark)

3 Write the words below adding the correct **prefix** from the box.

in	im	il	ir

a) excusable ______________ e) legal ______________

b) pertinent ______________ f) logical ______________

c) reverent ______________ g) possible ______________

d) perfect ______________ h) direct ______________

3 (1 mark)

! Top tips

- When a word begins with *dis*, you can usually remove the *dis* and a root word will still exist. When a word begins with *des*, it doesn't usually make sense if you remove *des*.
- Remember to keep the double letter if the prefix ends and the word begins with the same letter.
- Prefixes have different meanings: *re* = again or back *sub* = under *inter* = between *super* = above *anti* = against *auto* = self

/3

Total for this page

Suffixes: *-tion*, *-ssion*, *-cian*

To achieve 100+ you need to correctly spell words containing these suffixes.

1 Sort the words below into four groups and then add them to the table, including the correct **suffix**.

apprehend permit express persuade politic divert
exhibit possess electric ascend decide extend
inject confuse

Ends in d, de or se	Ends in c or cs	Ends in ss or mit	Ends in another way

1 (2 marks)

2 Select the correct spellings in the sentences below. Write the correct word on the line.

a) This story contains too much **repetition / repeatition**.

____

b) There will need to be considerable **adaption / adaptation** to make this building suitable for a wheelchair.

____

c) There was a huge **expulsion / expelsion** of gases from the volcano.

____

d) The scientist, Charles Darwin, developed a theory about **evolution / evolvution**.

____

2 (1 mark)

! Top tips

- *-tion* is the most common ending to make the sound 'shun'.
- *-sion* is used if the word ends in *d*, *de* or *se*. Remove the final *d*, *de* or *se* and add *-sion*.
- *-cian* is used if the word ends in *c* or *cs*.
- *-ssion* is used if the root word ends in *ss* or *mit*.
- Remember to remove the final letter before the suffix, if necessary.

/3 Total for this page

Suffixes: *-ous, -tious, -cious*

To achieve 100+ you need to correctly spell words containing these suffixes.

1 Draw lines to link the words with similar meanings.

1 (1 mark)

boisterous	well-mannered
callous	hard-hearted
carnivorous	lively
conscious	awake
cautious	meat-eating
momentous	important
courteous	careful

2 Write a sentence using each of the words below. Remember to punctuate your answers correctly.

2 (4 marks)

infectious ______________________________

religious ______________________________

notorious ______________________________

outrageous ______________________________

3 Remind yourself of the rule for words ending in y.

3 (1 mark)

Add the **suffix** -ous to the words below, making any necessary changes.

fury ______________

vary ______________

glory ______________

study ______________

injury ______________

/6 Total for this page

Suffixes: *-able, -ably, -ible, -ibly*

To achieve 100+ you need to correctly spell words containing these suffixes.

1 Add the words from the box to the sentences below.

unreachable	**unintelligible**	**plausible**	**edible**	**irreversible**

a) That's a ________________ suggestion and it may work.

b) The island was ________________ by boat because of the storm.

c) The radio signal was so poor that the voice was ________________.

d) Some fungi are ________________ but some are poisonous.

e) Once you have accepted the decision, it will be ________________.

1 *(1 mark)*

2 Spot the spelling mistakes in the passage below. Underline them and write the correct spellings on the lines below.

The small child was almost unnoticable until she stepped into the spotlight and began to climb the pole to the trapeze swing. The crowd were understandably hushed, probibly through anxiety that she may fall. It was unbelieveble to see how flexable she was, curling around the swing like a cat.

________________ ________________

________________ ________________

2 *(2 marks)*

3 The words below have to be changed before the **suffix** -able is added. Make the change and add the **suffix**.

classify ________________ envy ________________

identify ________________ glorify ________________

rely ________________ pity ________________

Write each word in a sentence.

____

____

____

____

____

____

3 *(6 marks)*

/9 *Total for this page*

Suffixes: *-ant, -ance, -ancy, -ent, -ence, -ency*

To achieve 100+ you need to correctly spell words containing these suffixes.

1 Match these words with the one most **similar** in meaning.

preference	life
advance	choice
magnificent	go forwards
conference	wonderful
existence	meeting
incompetence	failure

1 (1 mark)

2 Select the words from the box to complete the sentences.

absent audience diligently performance interference persistently

Although Nisha had been ________________ from the rehearsals, she had ________________ learned her lines ready for the ________________. However, one member of the ________________ was causing great ________________ in the show as he was ________________ calling out the endings to Nisha's jokes.

2 (1 mark)

3 Circle the correct spelling.

transparant	transparent
acquaintance	acquantence
resistence	resistance
perseverence	perseverance
vigilent	vigilant
insignificant	insignificent

3 (1 mark)

/3 Total for this page

Words with *ie, ei, eigh, ey, ay*

To achieve 100+ you need to correctly spell words containing these combinations of letters.

1 Add ie or ei to the words below.

a) What a super ach______vement.

b) It is not conven______nt to see you now.

c) We can get a cour______r to deliver the urgent parcel.

d) My n______ce is two tomorrow.

e) The fire is burning f______rcely.

1 (1 mark)

2 Organise these words into two groups within the table.

ceiling alien protein counterfeit hygienic deceitful

relieve Einstein foreigner height field heiress

ei words	ie words

2 (2 marks)

3 Complete the sentences below using words from the table.

a) A female who inherits is an ______________.

b) Fake money is ______________.

c) A famous scientist: Albert ______________.

d) Keeping things clean is ______________.

e) If you visit another country, you will be a ______________.

3 (1 mark)

/4 Total for this page

Words with *ough*

To achieve 100+ you need to correctly spell words containing this combination of letters.

1 Complete the sentences using the ough words in the box.

drought boughs afterthought enough hiccoughs wrought

a) I have ______________ sweets for everyone.

b) Some ______________ were damaged in last night's storm.

c) I have a terrible case of the ______________.

d) The gate to the castle was made of ______________ iron.

e) 'Thank you,' said Tom as an ______________.

f) The lack of rain is causing a dreadful ______________.

1 (1 mark)

2 Match each ough word with a suffix from the box and write the new word on the line.

en ful ness est

rough ______________ thorough ______________

tough ______________ thoughtful ______________

2 (1 mark)

3 Use the dictionary to help you match these unusual ough words with their meanings.

brougham	a period of leave for a soldier
thoroughfare	a roadway
doughty	hardy, brave
furlough	a type of horse-drawn carriage
slough off	a type of racehorse
thoroughbred	get rid of

3 (1 mark)

/3 Total for this page

Word endings: *al, el , il, le*

To achieve 100+ you need to correctly spell words that end with these letters.

1 Match the words with similar meanings.

anvil	a type of bag
uncivil	impolite
abnormal	a blacksmith's tool
cardinal	a high-status job in the church
admiral	an officer in the navy
satchel	unusual

1 (1 mark)

2 Complete the words by adding the correct two letters.

foss_ _
aeri_ _
applicab_ _
coast_ _
presidenti_ _
profession_ _
icic_ _
sentiment_ _

carous_ _
mythic_ _
barr_ _
terrib_ _
parall_ _
archaeologic_ _
squirr_ _

2 (1 mark)

3 Complete the sentences below with the correct word from the box.

criminal audible carousel peril

Please speak up as you are barely ________________.

A ________________ is someone who will break the law.

Be careful. You are in ________________ of falling off the cliff.

We will have a ________________ of activities that change each hour.

3 (1 mark)

/3 Total for this page

Silent letters

To achieve 100+ you need to correctly spell words containing silent letters.

1 Circle the **silent letter** in each word.

1 (1 mark)

a) handkerchief
b) scene
c) scissors
d) hymn
e) crumb
f) fascinate
g) campaign
h) solemn
i) guilt

2 Add the missing **silent letter** to the words below.

2 (1 mark)

a) w_istle
b) g_ess
c) _nome
d) tom_
e) cres_ent
f) desi_n
g) san_wich
h) lis_en
i) _nowledge
j) rog_e

3 Write sentences that include the pairs of words below. Remember to punctuate your answers correctly.

3 (5 marks)

a) anchor glistening

____

b) rustle doubt

____

c) stomach aches

____

d) sword knight

____

e) wretched solemn

____

/7 Total for this page

Homophones

To achieve 100+ you need to correctly spell a variety of homophones.

1 Write the correct spelling of the word that is used incorrectly.

a) What have you written on the bored?

____

b) A dessert can get very cold at night.

____

c) We except all clothing donations as long as they are in bags.

____

d) The cue for the favourite ride at the fair was very long.

____

e) The traffic was stationery for an hour.

____

1 (1 mark)

2 Write the **homophone** for the words given below.

loan	________	alter	________
maid	________	seam	________
bawled	________	sighed	________
bear	________	sole	________

2 (1 mark)

3 Select a word from the box to complete the sentences.

maize maze missed mist seize sees sort sought sheikh shake

a) The ____________ is ripening in the sun and will soon be ready to pick.

b) A ____________ was falling across the valleys.

c) Joe took the opportunity to ____________ the rugby ball and run with it.

d) What ____________ of car is your favourite?

e) Give the rug a good ____________ to remove the dust.

3 (1 mark)

/3 Total for this page

Synonyms and antonyms

To achieve 100+ you need to know the terms synonym and antonym, and identify examples.

1 Tick the word **closest** in meaning to <u>concur</u>.

agree ☐ conquer ☐
argue ☐ cure ☐

1 (1 mark)

2 Draw a line to match each word to its opposite meaning.

wandering	abandon
aggressive	direct
achieve	pacifying
durable	weak

2 (1 mark)

3 Which word is the **antonym** of <u>deny</u>?

attempt ☐ invite ☐
confirm ☐ recognise ☐

3 (1 mark)

4 Which word is a **synonym** of <u>antiquated</u>?

old-fashioned ☐
half-hearted ☐
open-minded ☐
sharply dressed ☐

4 (1 mark)

5 Match the words below with their **synonyms**.

comply	persuade
coerce	agree
corrupt	organise
collate	destroy

5 (1 mark)

! Top tip

- Remember: *S* for synonym, *S* for same. *A* for antonym, *A* for against.

/5 Total for this page

Word families

To achieve 100+ you need to know words which share the same root word or prefix.

1 Tick the words that belong to the same **word family**.

correction ☐
correspondent ☐
correspondence ☐
core ☐

1 (1 mark)

2 Write the root word for this **word family**.

delivery deliverable

____

2 (1 mark)

3 Add another word to this **word family**.

improve improving

____

3 (1 mark)

4 What does the root cover mean in the **word family** below?

discovery **covering** **uncover**

Tick **one**.

clothe ☐
hide ☐
make ☐
reveal ☐

4 (1 mark)

5 Write a sentence using the word curve as a **noun**. Remember to punctuate your answer correctly.

____

5 (1 mark)

6 Write a sentence using the word curve as a **verb**. Remember to punctuate your answer correctly.

____

6 (1 mark)

/6 Total for this page